12 Great Songs

BY GOSPEL MUSIC HALL OF FAME SONGWRITER

Mosie Lister

ARRANGED FOR CHOIR BY RICHARD KINGSMORE

Lillenas PUBLISHING COMPANY

KANSAS CITY, MO 64141

Contents

Then I Met the Master

Words and Music by
MOSIE LISTER
Arranged by Richard Kingsmore

found me;_____ A new day broke through all a-

round me;_____ For I met the

Mas - ter;_____ Now I be - long to

You Are My Song

Words and Music by
MOSIE LISTER
Arranged by Richard Kingsmore

in - to my heart one morn - ing;_____ My

world came a - live when I heard the mel - o - dy._____

Duet

_____ The Sun broke thro',____ and a brand new day____ came

18

I Won't Turn Back

Words and Music by
MOSIE LISTER
Arranged by Richard Kingsmore

nev - er let me fall. I mean to stay be -

side Him 'til I reach heav-en-ly ground.
I mean to stay on heav-en-ly ground. I won't

look to the left,_____ look to the right,_____ and nev-er-more turn a-round,_____

36

Where No One Stands Alone

Words and Music by
MOSIE LISTER
Arranged by Richard Kingsmore

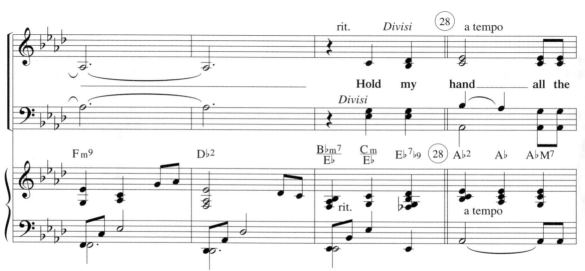

44

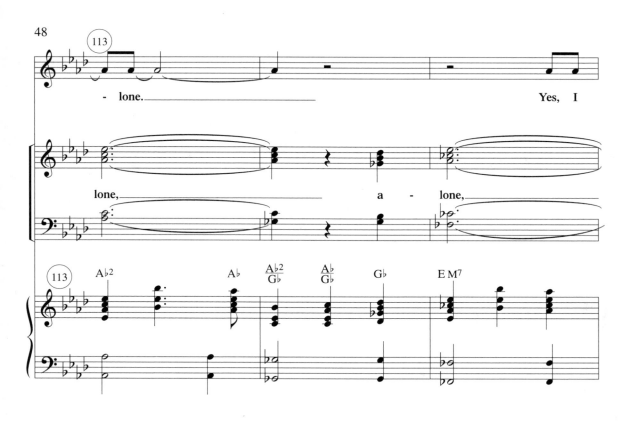

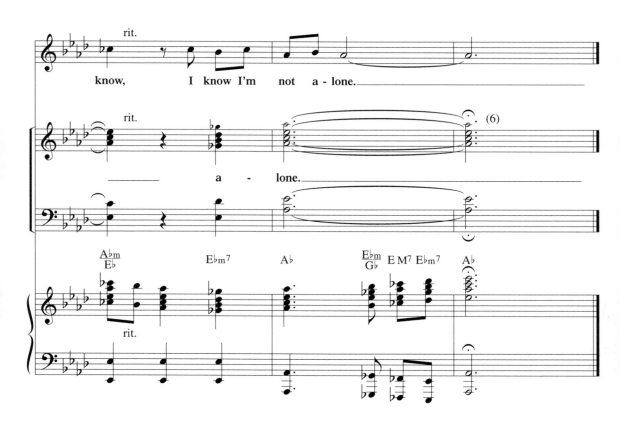

Let Some Drops Fall on Me

with

There Shall Be Showers of Blessing

Words and Music by
MOSIE LISTER
Arranged by Richard Kingsmore

PLEASE NOTE: Copying of this product is not covered by CCLI licenses. For CCLI information call 1-800-234-2446.

CD: 31

*"There Shall Be Showers of Blessing"

send - ing show'rs of bless - ing, Let some drops, Lord, fall on

me. Let there be show - ers of

bless - ing, Show - ers of bless - ing we need.

CD: 33

Basses only

Bless me, Je - sus, Let the show - ers____ fall.

drops, Lord, fall on me.

Bless me, Je - sus, Let the show - ers___ fall,

Let some drops, Lord, fall on___

me!

Holy Lamb of God

Words and Music by
MOSIE LISTER
Arranged by Richard Kingsmore

In this ho - ly place we bow to - day and

60

love _____ You. You are Lord of ev - 'ry - thing we are. Ho - ly

Unison

Lamb of God, we __ love __ You.

CD: 36

Ho - ly Prince of Peace, Em -

64

Higher on the Mountain

Words and Music by
MOSIE LISTER
Arranged by Richard Kingsmore

Lyrics:
I've turned my face to the hill-side,
reach-ing to the sun-light of God's e-ter-nal

72

One of Your Children Needs You, Lord

Words and Music by
MOSIE LISTER
Arranged by Richard Kingsmore

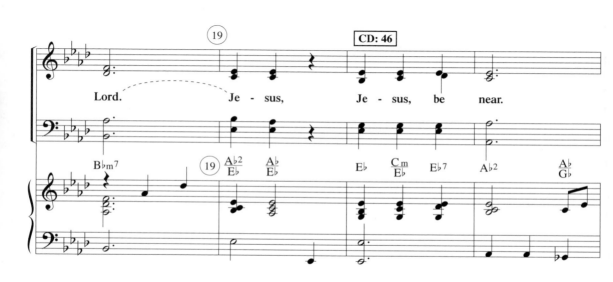

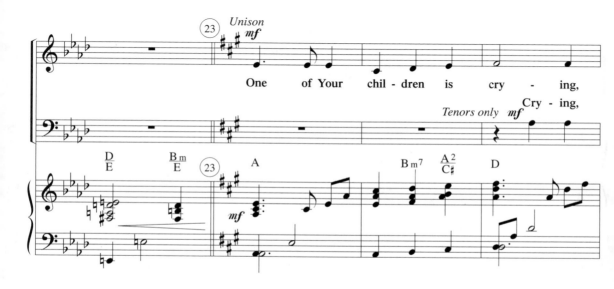

Take Me to the Fountain

with
Nothing but the Blood

Words and Music by
MOSIE LISTER
Arranged by Richard Kingsmore

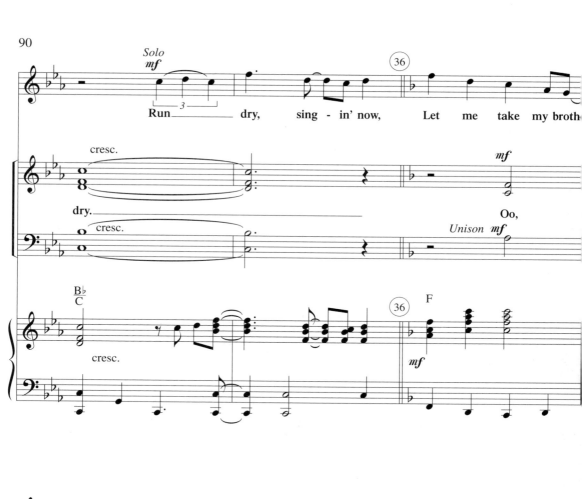

take me to the foun - tain,_____ To the liv - ing foun- tain_____ that nev - er shall run dry.

dry.

Je - sus is the foun-

Call Home

Words and Music by
MOSIE LISTER
Arranged by Richard Kingsmore

Ladies unison

There is a mo - ment

104

While Ages Roll

with

O That Will Be Glory

Words and Music by
MOSIE LISTER
Arranged by Richard Kingsmore

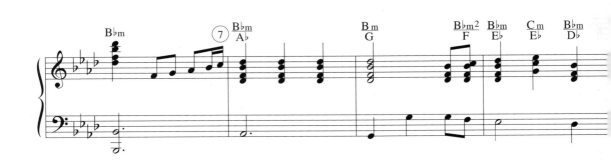

And while the a - ges

roll, I'll keep on prais - ing Him, And my

voice will nev - er tire or grow old.

And my song shall ev - er be, "Praise the

114

121

124

When They Call My Name

Words and Music by
MOSIE LISTER
Arranged by Richard Kingsmore

CD: 80

When they

Noth - ing to lose_____ and ev - 'ry - thing to gain,_____

ev - 'ry - thing to gain,_____

C

F⁶   E♭⁶   D⁷

call   my   name.   When they call   my

When they call   my   name.   When they call   my

G⁹   C¹³   F   Cm/E♭   D⁷   G⁹   C¹³

136